Peter Rabbit's

COOKERY BOOK

*Especially for
Ashleigh's
first Easter
love Vickie*

Peter Rabbit's
COOKERY BOOK

compiled by Anne Emerson

FREDERICK WARNE

ISBN 0 7232 2704 7

Typeset by CCC, printed and bound in Great Britain by
William Clowes Limited,
Beccles and London

D7205.1183

Before You Begin

'Mrs Tittlemouse was a most terribly tidy particular little mouse'—and if you want to be a popular cook who is always welcome in the kitchen, you would be wise to follow her example.

Always wear a clean apron to protect your clothes. Make sure that the table top or work surface and all your utensils are spotlessly clean. Always wash your hands and scrub your nails before you start to cook, and again if they get sticky while you are cooking. Don't forget to do the washing up. If you are waiting for something to cook in the oven you can fill in the time by washing up the utensils you have already used.

Don't be too proud to ask for help, particularly if you have never cooked before. An adult will be pleased to turn on an oven or a cooking ring or the grill on the stove for you. Gas jets should always be lit by an adult. Remember that an oven must be given time to heat before you put things into it to cook, so make sure that it is turned on to the right temperature 15 minutes before you need it.

To be on the safe side, ask a grown-up to put your

cooking into the oven for you, and to take it out again when it is ready. **Remember that anybody touching hot things in an oven, or even just opening the oven door, must wear oven gloves.**

If you have an eye-level grill on your stove, then an adult must do the grilling part of a recipe for you. Boiling kettles can be a tricky business too, and pouring the hot water (and also hot milk and gravy from saucepans) should be done by an older person. Saucepan handles should be turned inwards on the stove to prevent people knocking into them and tipping over the saucepans. If you have an electric kettle which you are going to boil yourself, make sure that your hands are perfectly dry before you touch the switch.

Perhaps you would prefer an adult to slice or chop vegetables for you too, but if you are going to do this job yourself ask which knife would be safe for you to use, and be very careful with it.

Once you have decided what you are going to cook, read through the recipe so that you know exactly what you are going to do. This is so important that there is a reminder in every recipe. Collect all the things you will need before you start: the ingredients which are listed at the beginning of each recipe, and the utensils which are in heavy black letters in the instructions. You must also have kitchen scales and a measuring jug for measuring amounts. Both metric and imperial (in brackets) measurements are given—follow the one you are familiar with.

Don't forget to warm the plates if you are serving hot food. You can put them in a low oven for a few minutes, or plunge them into a bowl of warm water, just before serving. Dry them well.

The recipes have been arranged in the following groups: for a party, for breakfast and for lunch or supper; but you can switch some of them around if you like. Jane Doll Cook's Golden Jelly would make an excellent pudding or it could be eaten for tea, and so could Mrs Rabbit's Currant Buns and Appley Dapply's Jam Tarts. And what about Bread and Milk and Blackberries for breakfast instead of supper?

I hope you will enjoy making and eating the food in this book. But should you happen to overeat yourself, like Peter Rabbit, here's how to make Camomile Tea.

Take one camomile tea bag and put it in a cup. Pour boiling water into the cup. Leave for 3 minutes . . . and by this time I am sure you will be feeling so *very* much better that you won't have to drink it after all!

Pig-wig's Conversation Peppermints

ingredients (*about 50 mints*)
250 g (10 oz) icing sugar
1 small egg (use the white)
peppermint essence

method
1 Read through the recipe and collect the utensils.
2 **Sieve** the icing sugar into a **basin**.
3 Crack the egg on the edge of the basin and empty on to a **plate**.
4 Turn an **egg cup** upside down over the yolk, and holding it firmly, tilt the plate over a **mixing bowl**. Only the egg white will run into the bowl.
5 Whisk the egg white with a **fork** until it is frothy.
6 Begin to add the icing sugar to the egg white, a **tablespoon** at a time. Mix each spoonful well into the white of the egg with a **wooden spoon**.
7 When you have added three-quarters of the icing sugar,

8

pour in very carefully 6 drops of peppermint essence. Mix well and taste. Add more if necessary.

8   Continue adding the icing sugar until the mixture is no longer sticky. Knead it into a soft ball.

9   Wash your hands and dry them well.

10a Sprinkle a little icing sugar on to a **pastry board**. Put the ball on the board and gently press out flat with your hands until it is about 5 mm ($\frac{1}{4}$ in) thick. Cut out peppermints with a **small round sweet cutter**.

10b *Or* another way to make peppermints is to take a pinch of the mixture from the ball and roll it into a soft marble in your hands. Pat with your fingers to flatten it.

11 Cover a **large plate** with **waxed paper**, sprinkle on some icing sugar and arrange the peppermints on it.

12 After 30 minutes, take a **clean pin** and prick a letter of the alphabet on each peppermint. Leave out X, Y and Z.

13 Leave overnight until the peppermints are crisp.

These are party starters. Ask your guests to take a peppermint and a partner. They must carry on a conversation for 5 minutes, using as many words beginning with the letter on their peppermint as they can. The winner eats both mints.

Jeremy Fisher's Butterfly Sandwiches

ingredients
8 slices of white or brown bread
(firm slices 10 mm ($\frac{1}{2}$ in) thick)
butter for spreading
about 100 g (4 oz) cream cheese
4 medium-size carrots
4 small gherkins

method
1   Read through the recipe and collect the utensils.
2   Wash and scrape the carrots with a **vegetable peeler**.
3   Cut off the tops and tails with a **kitchen knife**. Then cut each carrot into 8 rings about 5 mm ($\frac{1}{4}$ in) thick. Slice the gherkins down the middle and put them and the carrots on a **plate**.
4   Butter the slices of bread thinly with a **knife**.
5   Carefully cut out two equal triangles from each slice of bread, one from the top and one from the bottom, as

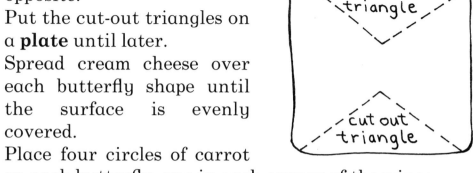

shown in the illustration opposite.

6   Put the cut-out triangles on a **plate** until later.

7   Spread cream cheese over each butterfly shape until the surface is evenly covered.

8   Place four circles of carrot on each butterfly, one in each corner of the wings.

9   Place a piece of gherkin along the centre of each butterfly to make a body.

10   Spread cream cheese on the left-over triangles. Put two triangles together to make a covered sandwich. Do the same with the others.

11   Arrange the butterflies and triangles prettily on a **large flat plate**.

other suggestions for butterfly sandwiches
Meat paste, cucumber rings, slivers of celery for bodies.
Sandwich spread, radish rings, strips of ham for bodies.
Honey sprinkled with currants, a line of raisins for bodies.
Chocolate spread, banana rings, orange segments for bodies.

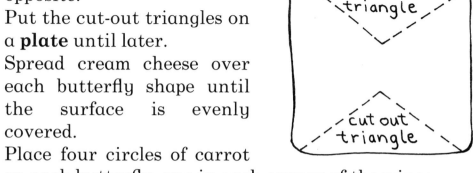
(illustration: square with text "cut out triangle" at top and "cut out triangle" at bottom)

11

Jane Doll Cook's Golden Jelly

ingredients (for 6 people)
1 packet orange jelly cubes
1 small tin mandarin oranges
1 small carton whipping cream
about $\frac{1}{4}$ litre ($\frac{1}{2}$ pint) water

method
1   Read through the recipe and collect the utensils.
2   Put some water in a **kettle** and put on to boil.
3   Pull apart the jelly cubes and put into a **measuring jug**.
4   When the kettle has boiled pour about $\frac{1}{4}$ litre ($\frac{1}{2}$ pint) of water carefully over the jelly cubes. Stir with a **dessert-spoon** until all the cubes have completely melted.
5   Wait 10 minutes to allow the jelly to cool.
6   Open the tin of mandarins with a **tin opener**. Stir the fruit and liquid into the jelly.

7   Rinse out a **round jelly mould** *or* **bowl** with cold water and pour in the jelly and fruit from the jug. Stir and leave in a cool place to set.

8   When the jelly is firm dip the mould into a **bowl** of hot water for about 5 seconds.

9   Ease the sides of the jelly away from the mould with your fingers.

10 Place a **large plate** on top of the mould, and holding it in place with one hand and the mould with the other, turn the mould upside down on the plate.

11 Hold the mould on the plate firmly and give it a sharp shake downwards. Lift off the mould.

12 The jelly should turn out whole on the plate.

13 Empty the carton of cream into a **basin** and whisk with a **hand whisk** until the cream is thick.

14 Fill a **piping bag** fitted with a **round nozzle** with cream and squeeze blobs of cream round the base of the jelly. Make a star shape in cream on the top. (You can make a piping bag by folding a greaseproof sandwich bag diagonally in half to make a cone. Cut off the pointed end, open out the cone and fill with cream. Squeeze out the cream.)

Mrs Rabbit's Currant Buns

ingredients (about 12 buns)
200 g (8 oz) self-raising flour
pinch of salt
75 g (3 oz) margarine
50 g (2 oz) caster sugar
1 egg
about 2 tablespoons of milk
50 g (2 oz) currants.

method
1   Read through the recipe and collect the utensils.
2   **Sieve** the flour and salt into a **mixing bowl.**
3   Hold the margarine over the mixing bowl, and cut into pieces with a **blunt knife.**
4   Rub the pieces of margarine into the flour with your finger tips until it is like fine breadcrumbs.
5   Add the sugar and currants, mixing well with a **fork.**

6   Crack the egg on the side of a **basin** and empty it into the basin. Whisk with a fork until it is bubbly.

7   Add the beaten egg gradually to the ingredients in the mixing bowl, stirring with a fork. Add the milk gradually, stirring well. The mixture should be stiff and ready to drop off the fork.

8   Take a small piece of **greaseproof paper** and rub it over some margarine or cooking fat. Rub the greased paper all over the surface of a **baking sheet**.

9   Take a level **dessertspoon** of mixture and heap it on to the sheet, with the help of a **teaspoon** to scrape off the mixture. Leave about 50 mm (2 in) between each bun to allow for spreading.

10   The baking sheet should be put in a hot oven (Electric 425°F or 220°C, or Gas No. 7) and baked for about 15 minutes or until the buns are brown.

11   When the baking sheet has been taken out of the oven, slip a **palette knife** under each bun and lift on to a **wire tray** to cool.

Appley Dapply's Jam Tarts

ingredients (12–14 tarts)
200 g (8 oz) plain flour
pinch of salt
50 g (2 oz) margarine
50 g (2 oz) lard
2–3 tablespoons cold water
jar of strawberry jam

method
1 Read through the recipe and collect the utensils.
2 **Sieve** the flour and salt into a **mixing bowl**.
3 Rub the margarine and lard into the flour with your finger tips until it looks like fine breadcrumbs.
4 Pour in a little water, and mix well with a **palette knife**.
5 Continue to add the water, mixing well, until the mixture forms a firm dough. Knead into a ball. (This is the method for short crust pastry.)
6 Sprinkle a **pastry board** and **rolling pin** with a little flour.

7　Place the pastry in the centre of the board and roll out until it is about 5 mm ($\frac{1}{4}$ in) thick.

8　Take a **round pastry cutter** and cut out as many circles from the rolled out pastry as you can.

9　Knead the pastry scraps together and roll out again. Cut out more circles.

10　Grease a **patty tin** (see page 15, No. 8), making sure that each compartment is well covered.

11　Lay a circle of pastry in each compartment. Press the pastry into the compartment with your fingers.

12　Put a level **teaspoon** of jam in the centre of each pastry tart.

13　Bake in a hot oven (Electric 425°F, 220°C or Gas No. 7) for about 20 minutes or until the pastry is golden brown.

14　When the patty tin has been taken out of the oven slip a palette knife under the tarts and place them on a **wire tray** to cool.

Ginger and Pickles' Oat Biscuits

ingredients (about 14 biscuits)
125 g (5 oz) self-raising flour
75 g (3 oz) porridge oats
75 g (3 oz) sugar
$\frac{1}{2}$ teaspoon bicarbonate of soda
50 g (2 oz) margarine
50 g (2 oz) lard
1 tablespoon golden syrup

method
1   Read through the recipe and collect the utensils.
2   **Sieve** the flour into a **basin** and add the oats, sugar and the bicarbonate of soda. Mix them together with a **wooden spoon**.
3   Put the margarine, lard and the golden syrup into a **medium-size saucepan** and put on a cooking ring which has been turned on to a low heat. Stir with a wooden spoon for a few minutes until the ingredients have melted.

18

4   Turn off the heat and add the dry ingredients from the basin. Stir with the wooden spoon until all the ingredients are well mixed.

5   Grease a **baking sheet** (see page 15, No. 8).

6   Take a rounded **dessertspoon** of the mixture and roll it into a ball about the size of a ping-pong ball in your hands. Place it on the baking sheet.

7   Continue in the same way until all the mixture is used. Leave about 75 mm (3 in) between each biscuit to allow for spreading. You may have to use two greased baking sheets.

8   Bake the biscuits in a medium oven (Electric 350°F or 180°C, or Gas No. 4) for about 20 minutes or until the biscuits are a golden brown.

9   When the biscuits have been taken out of the oven and have cooled a little, slip a **palette knife** under each one and lift on to a **wire tray**.

Your Very Good Health Lemonade

ingredients
2 large lemons
3 tablespoons honey
$\frac{1}{2}$ litre (1 pint) water
6 ice cubes

method
1 Read through the recipe and collect the utensils.
2 Pour the water into a **kettle** and put on to boil.
3 Wash the lemons under the cold water tap and dry them with a **clean tea towel**.
4 Cut the lemons into slices with a **saw-edged knife**.
5 Put them in a **large jug**, and add the honey.
6 When the kettle has boiled, turn off the heat. Take the

20

jug to the kettle and pour the water over the lemons and the honey.

7   Stir with a **tablespoon** to dissolve the honey. Press the spoon down on the lemon slices to squeeze out all the juice. Do this three or four times.

8   Cover the jug and let it stand for about an hour.

9   Take another **jug**, preferably a glass one, which will hold $\frac{1}{2}$ litre (1 pint) comfortably. Strain the lemonade through a **fine sieve** into this jug, leaving behind the lemon slices and the pips.

10   Add ice cubes to the lemonade and let it stand for two or three minutes, before serving.

This drink is very soothing if you have a cough or a sore throat, but do not put in the ice cubes.

Pigling Bland's Porridge

ingredients (for 2 or 3 people)
75 g (3 oz) porridge oats
2 cups of milk
brown sugar *or*
golden syrup to taste
pinch of salt

method
1 Read through the recipe and collect the utensils.
2 Put the milk in a **saucepan** and add the oats and salt.
3 Put the saucepan on a cooking ring which has been turned on to medium heat.
4 Bring to the boil, stirring all the time with a **wooden spoon**.
5 Lower the heat and cook gently for about 4 minutes, stirring, until it thickens. Turn off the heat.
6 Serve in bowls with sugar or golden syrup on top.

Mr McGregor's Porridge

ingredients (for 2 or 3 people)
75 g (3 oz) medium oatmeal
½ litre (1 pint) water
1½ teaspoons salt
about 4 tablespoons cold milk

method
1 Read through the recipe and collect the utensils.
2 Pour some water into a **kettle** and put on to boil.
3 When it is almost boiling put the oatmeal, salt and ¼ litre (½ pint) of cold water into a **saucepan**, and put on a cooking ring which has been turned on to medium heat. Stir with a **spirtle*** *or* the handle of a **wooden spoon**.
4 Pour in ¼ litre (½ pint) of boiling water, and bring it all to the boil, stirring all the time.
5 Lower the heat and cook gently, stirring occasionally, for 10 or 15 minutes until the porridge thickens.
6 Turn off the heat, and serve in bowls with cold milk.

* a spirtle is a Scottish porridge-stirring stick.

Bacon and Eggs, Bacon and Eggs!

ingredients (for 2 people)
3 lean rashers of bacon
3 eggs
25 g (1 oz) margarine
2 tablespoons milk
salt and pepper
2 slices of bread
butter for spreading

method
1   Read through the recipe and collect the utensils.
2   Make sure that the grill is turned on to medium heat.
3   Cut off the rind of the bacon with a **pair of scissors**. Cut out any gristly parts.
4   Put the rashers of bacon on the **grill pan tray** and place under the grill for about 3 minutes.
5   Remove the **grill pan** from the grill and turn the rashers

of bacon with **steak tongs** *or* a **fork**.

6 Grill the other side of the bacon for 3 minutes.

7 Remove the grill pan from the heat.

8 With a **kitchen knife** cut the bacon into small pieces on a **chopping board**.

9 Toast the slices of bread under the grill until both sides are a golden brown. Turn off the grill.

10 Crack the eggs on the rim of a **mixing bowl** and empty the contents into the bowl. Add the pepper and salt and the milk.

11 Whisk with a **fork** until the mixture is frothy.

12 Butter the slices of toast and put on **two breakfast plates**. Keep warm under the cooling grill.

13 Put the margarine into a **saucepan** and put over a low heat on the stove.

14 When the margarine has melted pour in the egg liquid. Stir with a **wooden spoon** until it begins to thicken.

15 Add the bacon pieces. Stir for a few seconds until the egg is creamy.

16 Turn off the cooking ring, and spoon out the scrambled egg on to the slices of toast. Serve immediately.

25

Peter Rabbit's Salad

ingredients (for 4 people)
1 small lettuce
1 cucumber
about 20 radishes
150 g (6 oz) white cabbage
$\frac{1}{4}$ of a small onion
2 tablespoons mayonnaise ⎫
2 tablespoons plain yogurt ⎭
or
4 tablespoons salad cream

method
1   Read through the recipe and collect the utensils.
2   Take a **kitchen knife** and cut off the root of the lettuce on a **chopping board**. Remove any outside leaves which are withered or marked. Break apart the lettuce, and if it has a heart cut it into four.
3   Cut out any thick white stalk from the piece of cabbage, and cut off the radish stalks and tails. Peel the onion.
4   Wash all the salad stuff well in cold water, drain in a

colander and dry in a **clean cloth**.

5 Cut the cabbage into thin slices so that it falls into shreds. Chop the shreds smaller if necessary.

6 Chop the onion quarter into tiny pieces.

7 Chop four radishes into tiny pieces.

8 Put the shredded cabbage, chopped onion and chopped radishes into a **bowl** and add the mayonnaise and yogurt, *or* the salad cream. Mix all together with a **wooden spoon**.

9 Arrange the lettuce equally on **four plates**, leaving a hole in the centre of each plate.

10 Cut off both ends of the cucumber, and slice the rest into thin circles. Arrange in a ring around the plate on top of the lettuce.

11 Cut the other radishes in half and place on top of the cucumber slices at equal distances apart.

12 Put a heaped **tablespoon** of the mixture from the bowl in the centre of each plate.

If you are serving Peter Rabbit's Salad as a side salad with another dish, serve in bowls.

The Sandy Whiskered Gentleman's Herb Omelette

ingredients (for 4 people)
6 eggs
1 tablespoon of cooking oil
25 g (1 oz) butter
1 sprig fresh parsley (*or* $\frac{1}{2}$ teaspoon dried parsley)
4 leaves of fresh thyme (*or* 1 pinch of dried thyme)
1 leaf of fresh mint (*or* a small pinch of dried mint)
pinch of salt
shake of pepper

method
1 Read through the recipe and gather the utensils.
2 If you are using fresh parsley, thyme and mint wash them in cold water. Cut off the stems with a **kitchen knife**.
3 Chop the leaves into tiny pieces on a **chopping board** and put them on a **plate**.

4   Crack each egg on the rim of a **medium mixing bowl** and empty the contents into the bowl.

5   Add the pepper and salt and whisk the eggs with a **hand whisk** until they are very frothy.

6   Turn a cooking ring on the stove to medium heat. Turn on the grill to high heat. Put **plates** in the oven turned on low to warm.

7   Melt the oil and butter in a **20 cm (8 in) frying pan** for about 3 minutes until it is hot.

8   Whisk the egg mixture again and pour it carefully into the pan on the stove.

9   When the bottom of the omelette begins to set but while the top is still runny, sprinkle in the chopped (or dried) herbs. Stir them into the runny egg gently with a **wooden spoon**.

10 Turn off the cooking ring, and put the pan under the grill to finish cooking. The top of the omelette should be fluffy and golden brown.

11 Turn off the grill and the oven and take out one warm plate. With the help of an **egg slice** slip the omelette on to the plate. Cut into wedges and serve immediately with Peter Rabbit's Salad, page 26.

Patty-pan Pie

ingredients (for 4 people)
200 g (8 oz) plain flour
50 g (2 oz) margarine
50 g (2 oz) lard
2–3 tablespoons cold water
1 tin stewed steak 425 g (15 oz)
pinch of salt

method
1 Read through this recipe and the recipe on pages 16–17 Nos. 2–6. Collect all the utensils.
2 Make pastry as described on pages 16–17, Nos. 2–6.
3 Roll out the pastry into a rectangle about 5 mm ($\frac{1}{4}$ in) thick, and about 50 mm (2 in) bigger all the way round than your **small pie dish**.
4 Instead of a **metal patty-pan** to hold up the pie crust, you can use a **pie funnel**, *or* an **oven proof ramekin dish** *or* **egg cup** (not plastic) turned upside down. Place

it in the centre of the pie dish.

5   Open the tin of stewed steak with a **tin opener** and empty the contents into the pie dish.

6   With a **knife** cut pastry strips about 10 mm ($\frac{1}{2}$ in) wide from the edges of the rolled out pastry.

7   Brush the pie dish rim with a **pastry brush** dipped in cold water. Lay the pastry strips along the rim, damping the edges where the strips overlap. Press the pastry down with your fingers.

8   Brush the pastry rim with water.

9   Lay the pastry lid over the pie dish so that the centre of the pastry covers the 'patty-pan' and the edges overlap the pie dish rim. Press round the rim with your fingers.

10   If you are using a pie funnel make a slit over the top with a knife, so that the tip pokes through the pastry. Otherwise make a slit in the pastry each side of the 'patty-pan'.

11   Trim off the overhanging pastry with the knife and press round the rim of the pie with a **fork**.

12   Bake in a hot oven (Electric 425°F or 220°C, or Gas No. 7) for about 30 minutes or until it is brown.

Robinson's Cauliflower Cheese and Egg

ingredients (for 4 people)
$\frac{3}{4}$ kg ($1\frac{1}{2}$ lb) cauliflower
1 tablespoon salt
4 eggs
100 g (4 oz) Cheddar cheese
25 g (1 oz) flour
1 level teaspoon mustard powder
$\frac{1}{4}$ litre ($\frac{1}{2}$ pint) milk
25 g (1 oz) margarine
shake of pepper

method
1 Read through the recipe and collect the utensils.
2 Half fill a **large plastic bowl** with cold water and add most of the salt, leaving about two pinches for flavouring.
3 Take a **kitchen knife** and cut off any green outside leaves and the stalk of the cauliflower on a **chopping**

board. Cut it into pieces and put in the bowl to soak.

4 Pour about ½ litre (1 pint) of cold water into a **medium saucepan,** add a pinch of salt, and put on a cooking ring turned to high heat to boil.

5 Put the eggs into a **small saucepan,** cover with cold water, and put on a cooking ring turned on to high heat to boil. They should boil for 10 minutes.

6 When the water in the medium saucepan is boiling put in the cauliflower pieces. They should boil for about 15 minutes.

7 While the eggs and cauliflower are cooking, start to make the cheese sauce. Grate the cheese on to a plate, using the large holes of a **grater.**

8 **Sieve** the flour, mustard powder, salt and pepper into a **medium mixing bowl,** and gradually add about a quarter of the milk, mixing with a **wooden spoon** until you have a smooth paste.

9 When the eggs have been boiling for 10 minutes, turn off the cooking ring. Empty out the hot water in the sink and run cold water over the eggs. Gently bash the ends and leave in more cold water to cool.

10 When the cauliflower has been boiling for about 15 minutes, test with a **fork.** The pieces should be tender

but not falling apart. Drain them in a **colander** in the sink.

11   Lay the cauliflower pieces in a **medium pie dish.**

12   Gently bash the eggs all over and peel off the shells. Cut the eggs in half down the centre on the chopping board, and place amongst the cauliflower.

13   Continue to make the sauce. Pour the rest of the milk into a **milk saucepan** and put over the cooking ring turned down to medium heat.

14   Heat the milk until it is just about to boil. Take it off the heat and pour into the basin over the mixture, stirring all the time to keep it from going lumpy.

15   Pour the sauce back into the saucepan, and put it on the cooking ring turned down to low. Stir it all the time until it boils. Continue to boil for 3 minutes, still stirring to stop it sticking.

16   Add the margarine and stir again.

17   Turn off the heat and stir in half the grated cheese.

18   Pour the sauce over the egg and cauliflower in the pie dish, and sprinkle the rest of the cheese on top.

19   Put the pie dish in a medium oven (Electric 350°F, or 180° C, or Gas No. 4) for about 20 minutes or until it is brown on top.

Gammon and Spinach! Ha Ha HA!

ingredients (for 4 people)
$\frac{3}{4}$ kg ($\frac{1}{2}$ lb) tender young spinach
100 g   (4 oz) half-gammon   *or*
back rashers of bacon (without rind)
2 tablespoons olive oil
1 tablespoon lemon juice
a sprinkling of salt and pepper

method
1   Read through the recipe and collect the utensils.
2   Wash the spinach very well and dry in a **clean cloth.**
3   Pull the leaves off the stems and break into small pieces.
4   Mix the oil, lemon juice, pepper and salt in a **salad bowl,** with a **wooden spoon.** Toss the spinach in this dressing.
5   Put the rashers under a medium grill and grill for about 3 minutes on both sides, turning with **steak tongs** or a **fork.**
6   Chop the bacon with a **knife** and mix in with the salad.

35

Gravy and Potatoes in a Good Brown Pot

ingredients (for 4 people)
¾ kg (1½ lb) medium-size potatoes
1 tin of steak about 425 g (15 oz)
½ beef stock cube
half a tin of cold water
100 g (4 oz) lean bacon

method
1   Read through the recipe and collect the utensils.
2   Wash the potatoes and peel them with a **potato peeler**.
3   Take a **kitchen knife** and slice the potatoes into thin
    oval slices on a **chopping board**.
4   Cut off the rind, gristle, and any fat from the bacon with
    a **pair of scissors**. Cut the bacon into strips.
5   Open the tin of steak with a **tin opener**, and empty the

36

contents into a **medium-size saucepan**.

6   Half fill the tin with cold water and pour over the steak. Sprinkle half a beef stock cube over the top. Stir well with a **wooden spoon**.

7   Put the saucepan over a cooking ring turned on to medium heat, and bring the contents to the boil, stirring all the time. Turn the cooking ring to low and simmer for a few minutes. Turn off the heat.

8   Take a **medium casserole** (a brown one if you have one) and line the bottom with one third of the slices of potato, overlapping each slice a little.

9   With a **tablespoon**, spoon out half the meat from the saucepan and lay it evenly over the potato.

10   Take half the amount of bacon and lay it in strips on top of the meat.

11   Put another layer of potatoes on top, cover with meat, then strips of bacon.

12   End with a top layer of potato slices, slightly overlapping each other. Pour the gravy from the saucepan down the side of the casserole.

13   Put the casserole uncovered in a medium oven (Electric 375°F or 190°C, or Gas No. 5) for about 1 hour or until the potatoes are brown on top and tender underneath.

Toad in the Hole

ingredients (for 4 people)
100 g (4 oz) plain flour
pinch of salt
1 egg
$\frac{1}{4}$ litre ($\frac{1}{2}$ pint) milk
$\frac{1}{2}$ kg (1 lb) sausages (pork or beef)
25 g (1 oz) lard

method
1   Read through the recipe and collect the utensils.
2   **Sieve** the flour and salt into a **mixing bowl.** Make a hole in the centre of the flour.
3   Crack the egg on the side of the bowl, and empty into the hole in the flour.
4   Mix in the flour with a **wooden spoon.**
5   Gradually add the milk, mixing with the wooden spoon.

Beat well until all lumps have disappeared. The batter mixture should be a smooth pale yellow liquid.

6   Arrange the sausages in a **large baking tin.** Cut the lard into pieces with a **blunt knife** and dot between the sausages.

7   Put the tin into a hot oven (Electric 425°F or 220°C, or Gas No. 7) for about 10 minutes.

8   When the tin has been taken out of the oven, beat the batter mixture again for about 5 seconds.

9   Pour the batter over the sausages in the tin.

10   Put the baking tin into the oven again. Cook for about 25 minutes or until the batter is crisp and golden, and the sausages are brown.

Hunca Munca's Rice Pudding

ingredients
40 g (1½ oz) short grain rice
½ litre (1 pint) milk
40 g (1½ oz) caster sugar
25 g (1 oz) butter
nutmeg (whole or in a carton)

method
1 Grease a **medium pie dish** with margarine (see page 15, No. 8).
2 Put the rice in a **sieve** and run cold water over it to clean it.
3 Put the rice in the pie dish and pour the milk over it.

4 Add the sugar and stir with a **wooden spoon**.

5 With a **blunt knife** cut the butter into small pieces and dot over the rice.

6 Take a **grater** and on the fine holes grate a little nutmeg evenly over the pudding—*or* if you have powdered nutmeg in a carton shake a little over the rice.

7 Bake the pudding in a fairly low oven (Electric 310°F or 150°C, or Gas No. 2) very slowly for at least two hours.

8 A brown skin will form on the top of the pudding.

9 When the pie dish has been taken out of the oven, lift up the edge of the skin very carefully with a fork, and spoon out a **teaspoon** of pudding on to a **plate**.

10 If the rice is soft and creamy then the pudding is ready. If the rice is still rather hard, put it back in the oven for about 30 minutes.

Tabitha Twitchit's Roly-Poly Pudding

ingredients (for 4 people)
200 g (8 oz) plain flour
pinch of salt
50 g (2 oz) margarine
50 g (2 oz) lard
2–3 tablespoons cold water
40 g (1½ oz) soft butter
50 g (2 oz) sugar
125 g (5 oz) mixed currants,
sultanas and raisins
4 tablespoons clear honey *or* jam
or custard (see page 44)

method
1. Read through this recipe and also the recipe on pages 16–17 Nos. 2–5. Collect all the utensils.
2. Make pastry as described on pages 16–17, Nos. 2–5.
3. Sprinkle a **pastry board** and **rolling pin** with flour and roll out the pastry into a rectangle about 5 mm (¼ in) thick.

4   Spread butter over the pastry with a **palette knife**, leaving a border about 20 mm (1 in) uncovered all the way round the edge.

5   Mix the sugar with one **teaspoon** of cold water, and spread over the buttered area with the palette knife.

6   Sprinkle the currants, sultanas and raisins over the buttered and sugared area.

7   Brush the pastry border with a **pastry brush** dipped in cold water.

8   Starting with a narrow side, roll up the pastry lightly. Press down all round the edges with your fingers to seal them.

9   Grease a **baking sheet** (see page 15, No. 8) and put the roly-poly in the centre.

10 Bake in a hot oven (Electric 450°F or 230°C, or Gas No. 8) for about 30 or 35 minutes, until the roly-poly is brown.

11 When it has been taken out of the oven, slip a palette knife under it and place it on a large warm plate.

12 Serve with honey or jam which has been warmed in a **saucepan** over a low heat, or with custard (see page 44).

Cousin Ribby's Custard

ingredients
2 tablespoons custard powder
1 tablespoon caster sugar
$\frac{1}{2}$ litre (1 pint) milk

method
1   Read through the recipe and collect the utensils.
2   Put the custard powder and the sugar in a **bowl**. Add two tablespoons of the milk and mix well with the **table-spoon**.
3   Put the rest of the milk in a **medium-size saucepan** and put over a cooking ring turned on to medium heat. Bring to boiling point and pour into the bowl, stirring well.
4   Pour the mixture back into the saucepan and bring to the boil, stirring all the time.
5   Pour into a **jug** and serve with Roly-Poly Pudding (page 42).

Bread and Milk and Blackberries

ingredients (for 3 people)
3 thick slices of white bread
brown sugar to taste
about $\frac{1}{4}$ litre ($\frac{1}{2}$ pint) milk
3 heaped tablespoons black-
berries (either fresh or tinned)

method
1   Read through the recipe and collect the utensils.
2   Cut the bread into small squares with a **knife** and put into three **bowls**.
3   Sprinkle with brown sugar.
4   Put the milk into a **small saucepan** and put over a cooking ring turned on to medium heat. Warm the milk but do not let it boil. Turn off the cooking ring.
5   Pour the milk over the bread in the bowls.
6   Sprinkle the blackberries over the top.

45

Acknowledgements

The illustrations from the *Peter Rabbit* series by Beatrix Potter included in this book are reproduced by the kind permission of Frederick Warne & Co. Ltd. Pictures on pages 1, 4, 14, 23, 26, 45 and on the front and back cover are from *The Tale of Peter Rabbit*; pages 15 and 46 from the privately printed edition of *The Tale of Peter Rabbit*; page 2 from *The Tale of Benjamin Bunny*; page 3 from *The Tale of the Flopsy Bunnies*; pages 8, 22, 24 and 25 from *The Tale of Pigling Bland*; page 10 from *The Tale of Mr Jeremy Fisher*; pages 12, 40 and 41 from *The Tale of Two Bad Mice*; page 16 from *Appley Dapply's Nursery Rhymes*; pages 17, 18 and 19 from *The Tale of Ginger and Pickles*; pages 20, 21, 38 and 39 from *The Tale of Mrs Tittlemouse*; page 28 from *The Tale of Jemima Puddle-Duck*; pages 30, 31 and 44 from *The Tale of the Pie and the Patty-pan*; page 32 from *The Tale of Little Pig Robinson*; page 34 from *The Story of Miss Moppet*; pages 35 and 36 from *Cecily Parsley's Nursery Rhymes*; and pages 42 and 43 from *The Tale of Samuel Whiskers*.

I am also very grateful to those friends and relations who were kind enough to supply recipes which have been adapted for use in this book, and I would like to thank others for their helpful hints, sound advice and bravery which extended beyond the call of duty.

Index